Learn to Draw

SPACE

MEDIA ENHANCED BOOKS

AV²
BY WEIGL™

ADDED VALUE • AUDIO VISUAL

www.av2books.com

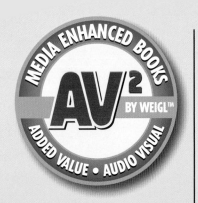

AV² provides enriched content that supplements and complements this book. Weigl's AV² books strive to create inspired learning and engage young minds in a total learning experience.

Your AV² Media Enhanced books come alive with...

 Audio
Listen to sections of the book read aloud.

 Video
Watch informative video clips.

 Embedded Weblinks
Gain additional information for research.

 Try This!
Complete activities and hands-on experiments.

 Key Words
Study vocabulary, and complete a matching word activity.

 Quizzes
Test your knowledge.

 Slide Show
View images and captions, and prepare a presentation.

... and much, much more!

Go to **www.av2books.com,** and enter this book's unique code.

BOOK CODE

T406321

AV² by Weigl brings you media enhanced books that support active learning.

Published by AV² by Weigl
350 5th Avenue, 59th Floor
New York, NY 10118
Website: www.weigl.com   www.av2books.com

Library of Congress Cataloging-in-Publication Data

Space / edited by Jordan McGill.
      p. cm. -- (Learn to draw)
 Includes index.
 ISBN 978-1-61690-859-1 (hardcover : alk. paper) -- ISBN 978-1-61690-865-2 (pbk. : alk. paper) -- ISBN 978-1-61690-989-5 (online)
 1. Outer space--In art--Juvenile literature. 2. Astronautics in art--Juvenile literature. 3. Drawing--Technique--Juvenile literature. I. McGill, Jordan.
 NC825.O9S66 2011
 743'.9962945--dc23
                              2011020315

Printed in the United States of America in North Mankato, Minnesota
1 2 3 4 5 6 7 8 9 0 15 14 13 12 11

062011
WEP290411

Project Coordinator: Jordan McGill
Art Director: Terry Paulhus

Every reasonable effort has been made to trace ownership and to obtain permission to reprint copyright material. The publishers would be pleased to have any errors or omissions brought to their attention so that they may be corrected in subsequent printings.

Weigl acknowledges Getty Images as its primary image supplier for this title.

Contents

6

10

14

18

22

26

Why Draw?

Drawing is easier than you think. Look around you. The world is made of shapes and lines. By combining simple shapes and lines, anything can be drawn. An orange is just a circle with a few details added. A flower can be a circle with ovals drawn around it. An ice cream cone can be a triangle topped with a circle. Most anything, no matter how complicated, can be broken down into simple shapes.

circle

oval

circle

circle

triangle

Drawing helps people make sense of the world. It is a way to reduce an object to its simplest form, say our most personal feelings and thoughts, or show others objects from our **imagination**. Drawing an object can help you learn how it fits together and works.

What shapes do you see in this car?

It is fun to put the world onto a page, but it is also a good way to learn. Learning to draw even simple objects introduces the skills needed to fully express oneself visually. Drawing is an excellent form of **communication** and improves people's imagination.

Practice drawing your favorite space objects in this book to learn the basic skills necessary to draw. You can use those skills to create your own drawings.

Space

Drawing objects from space and the technologies people have invented to study space is a great way to learn. You can learn about how the objects interact and what they do. Have fun drawing space technologies and space objects.

Outer space, often simply called space, is made up of almost empty regions of the universe beyond Earth. When we look up at the night sky, we mainly see tiny, twinkling lights that we call stars. They are just a small part of the universe. It is difficult to believe just how far away and how big those tiny lights are.

Human trips into space have taught people a great deal about space. However, the farthest humans have traveled is to the Moon. Some spacecrafts without pilots have traveled to the edge of our solar system. By learning more about the universe, we also learn more about ourselves and our own planet.

What is an Astronaut?

Astronauts are people trained to travel in a spacecraft and work in space. Astronauts cannot leave their spacecraft without spacesuits. These protective suits allow astronauts to stay in space for up to eight hours.

A spacesuit is a key piece of equipment for anyone heading into space. Astronauts wear these suits when they are lifting off from Earth, during landing, and anytime they are outside of their spacecraft in space. The suit provides protection when astronauts encounter the harsh environment found in space.

Helmet
The helmet keeps pressure at the right level to allow the astronaut to breathe. The front bubble is coated in a thin layer of gold to filter the Sun's harmful rays.

Control Panel
Using the control panel, an astronaut can control the **life support** systems of the suit.

Gloves
Space suit gloves are made of two main layers. The internal layer is like a rubber balloon surrounded by cloth, which keeps the gloves' shape. The outer layer protects the astronaut from **space debris** and extreme temperatures.

Life Support Systems
Worn like a backpack, the primary life support subsystem, or PLSS, provides astronauts with oxygen. It also filters out carbon dioxide, provides the astronaut with drinking water, and controls temperature.

White Top-Layer
Space suits are white because white reflects heat. This keeps astronauts cool. Temperatures under direct sunlight can reach more than 275 °Fahrenheit (135 °Celsius).

1 Start with a stick figure frame of the astronaut. Draw a circle for the head, ovals for the hands and feet, and lines for the body and limbs.

2 Now, draw the shape of the helmet and torso.

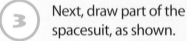

3 Next, draw part of the spacesuit, as shown.

4 Now, complete the spacesuit and draw the shoes.

5 In this step, add the jacket sleeves and draw the hands.

6 Draw the helmet screen and the backpack.

7 Now, add details to the spacesuit and the backpack, as shown.

8 Erase the extra lines and the stick figure.

9 Color the picture.

What are Moon Bases?

Scientists have begun to make plans for a lunar research station, or Moon base. Scientists could stay there for months, collecting data and performing experiments. The Moon base would need housing, laboratories, and lunar vehicles. All would be designed to support humans in a place where there is very little air and extreme temperatures.

Communication
Astronauts need to communicate with Earth while they are on the Moon. A communication system would allow them to maintain contact with Earth.

Expandable Design
A Moon base should grow over time. Most Moon base designs allow for additional structures to be added.

Habitation
A Moon base would need a place for scientists to live. It would contain sleeping quarters, showers, and a kitchen.

Power Storage
One part of the station would contain power storage units. They collect energy from the Sun and store it for use in the base. This provides energy for life support systems inside the base.

Surface Vehicle
A Moon base would need some form of transportation for scientists to travel on the Moon.

How to Draw a
Moon Base

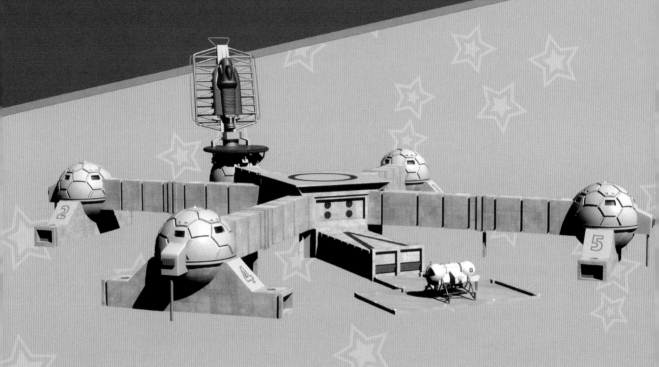

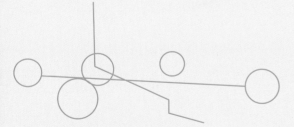

1 Start by drawing a stick figure frame of the Moon base. Use circles for the spheres, and lines for the body.

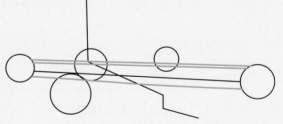

2 Now, draw three parallel lines across the figure, as shown.

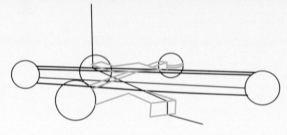

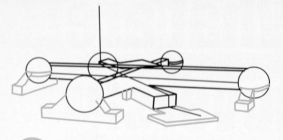

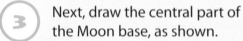

3 Next, draw the central part of the Moon base, as shown.

4 Next, draw the platforms, as shown.

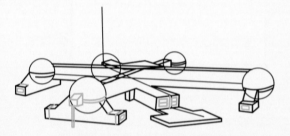

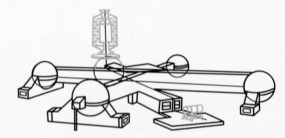

5 In this step, draw the remaining pieces, as shown.

6 Draw the antenna and a vehicle on the figure frame.

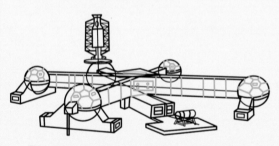

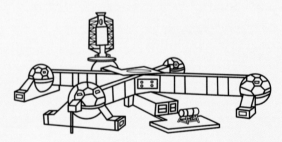

7 Now, add details to the spheres and central part, as shown.

8 Erase the extra lines and the stick figure.

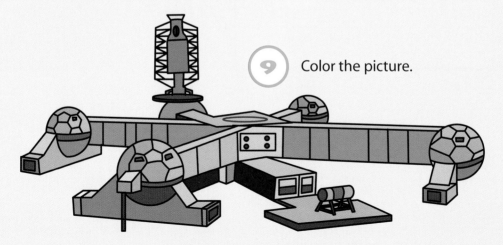

9 Color the picture.

What are Rovers?

The first rover to land on Mars was Sojourner in 1997. Sojourner's ability to move over the planet's surface allowed scientists to explore new places. Since then, two other rovers have landed successfully on Mars. The rovers gather information from different parts of the planet. This increases scientists' understanding of the planet's geology and the materials that form its surface. **NASA** plans to send two more rovers to Mars by 2019.

Antennae
The antennae allow scientists on Earth to send and receive information through a **radio system**.

Suspension
The wheels are connected to a suspension system that ensures the rover can move across rough terrain. The wheels can move up and down to cross gaps and rocky areas.

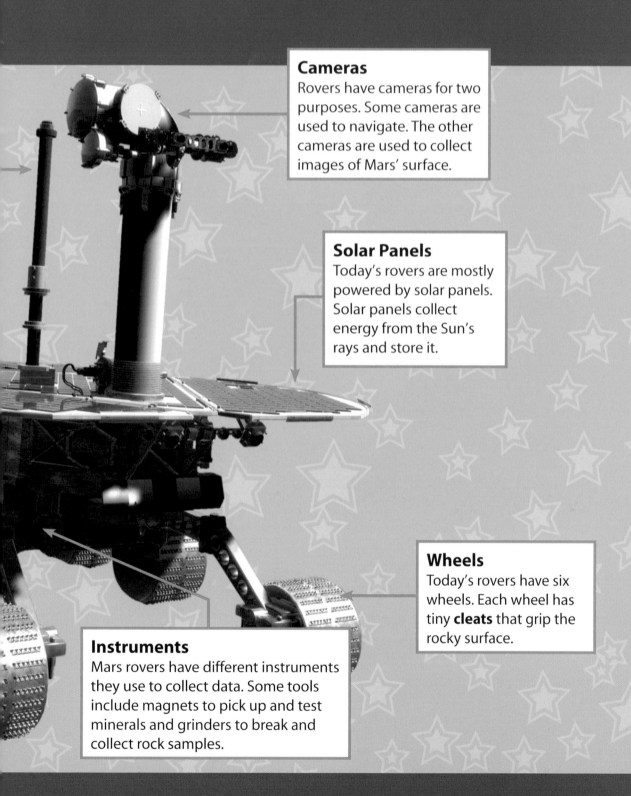

Cameras
Rovers have cameras for two purposes. Some cameras are used to navigate. The other cameras are used to collect images of Mars' surface.

Solar Panels
Today's rovers are mostly powered by solar panels. Solar panels collect energy from the Sun's rays and store it.

Wheels
Today's rovers have six wheels. Each wheel has tiny **cleats** that grip the rocky surface.

Instruments
Mars rovers have different instruments they use to collect data. Some tools include magnets to pick up and test minerals and grinders to break and collect rock samples.

How to Draw a Rover

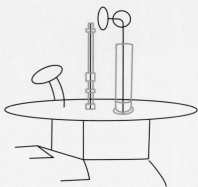

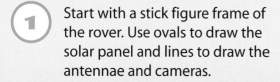

1 Start with a stick figure frame of the rover. Use ovals to draw the solar panel and lines to draw the antennae and cameras.

2 Now, add detail to the antenna on the line from the previous step, as shown.

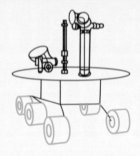

3 Next, draw the cameras and the other antenna.

4 Now, draw the wheels of the vehicle, as shown.

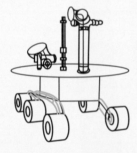

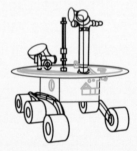

5 In this step, draw curved lines near the wheels, as shown.

6 Draw the details on the solar panel and other parts.

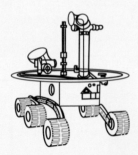

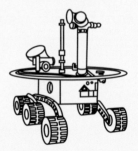

7 Now, draw small rectangles on the surface of the wheels.

8 Erase the extra lines and the stick figure.

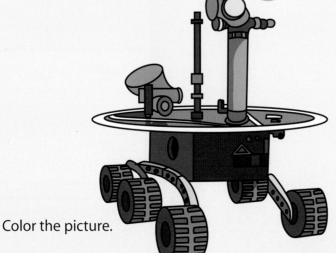

9 Color the picture.

What are Satellites?

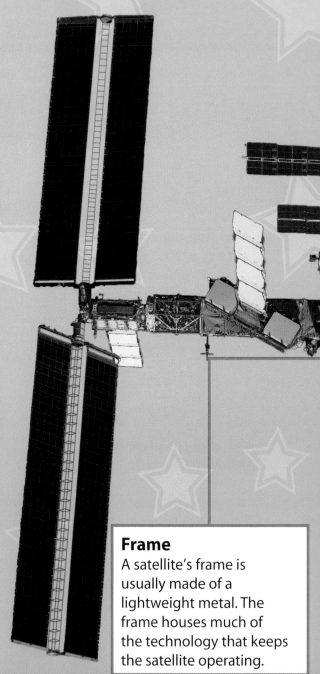

Satellites in **orbit** around Earth add to human knowledge of the planet. With satellites, scientists can study Earth from a distance and view large areas. Pictures from space provide information that helps explain why Earth looks the way it does and where changes are taking place. By studying Earth from both space and the ground, scientists can learn more about the ever-changing planet.

Frame
A satellite's frame is usually made of a lightweight metal. The frame houses much of the technology that keeps the satellite operating.

Onboard Computer

An onboard computer monitors the satellite's operating system. This system controls the satellite and tells it what to do.

Solar Panels

Solar panels provide most of the power needed to operate the satellite. They collect the Sun's energy and use it to power the satellite. Batteries on the frame make sure the satellite works when there is no sunlight.

Motor

Rocket motors move the satellite to a desired location. Many forces in space cause satellites to drift out of place. Forces that affect a satellite's positioning include solar wind and **gravity**. The motor system powers **thrusters** that can correct a satellite's positioning.

Antennae

Every satellite has a radio system with antennae. This system sends information to and from Earth.

How to Draw a Satellite

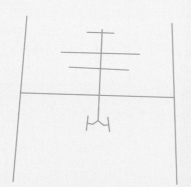

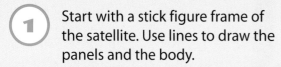

1 Start with a stick figure frame of the satellite. Use lines to draw the panels and the body.

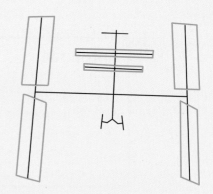

2 Draw the solar panels by drawing rectangles, as shown.

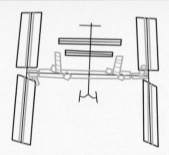

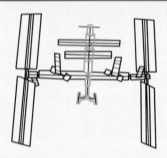

3 Next, draw the smaller panels and the main body, as shown.

4 Now, draw the antenna and cameras using cylinders and rectangles.

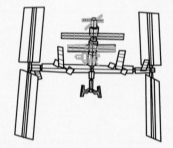

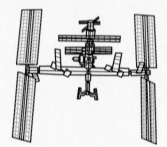

5 In this step, add details to the satellite, as shown.

6 Draw small lines on the solar panels.

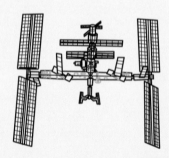

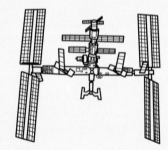

7 Next, draw small lines and circles on other parts of the satellite.

8 Erase the extra lines and the stick figure.

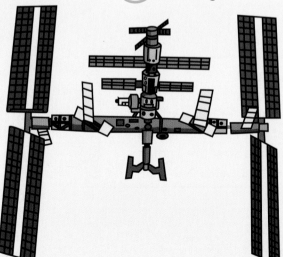

9 Color the picture.

What is the Solar System?

Earth is one of eight planets in our solar system. All of the planets travel around the Sun. Earth, Mars, Mercury, and Venus are called **terrestrial** planets. They consist mainly of rock. Jupiter, Neptune, Saturn, and Uranus are made up mostly of gas. They are called gas giants.

Sun
The Sun is the center of the solar system. The power of the Sun's gravity holds our solar system together. The Sun provides Earth with light, warmth, and a power source.

Mercury
The closest planet to the Sun, Mercury is only slightly larger than Earth's moon. Mercury is named after the Roman messenger god.

Venus
Venus is the brightest planet and can sometimes be seen with the naked eye. Venus is named after the Roman goddess of love and beauty.

Mars
The second-closest planet to Earth, Mars is home to the largest volcano in our solar system. Mars is named after the Roman god of war.

Jupiter
Jupiter is the largest planet in our solar system. It is so big that all the other planets in our solar system could fit inside of it. Jupiter is named after the Roman king of the gods.

Neptune
Neptune has a large dark spot about the size of Earth. The dark spot is actually a giant storm. Neptune is named after the Roman god of the sea.

Saturn
Saturn is known for its colorful rings. Even though it is the second biggest planet, it is the lightest. Saturn is named after the Roman god of farming.

Uranus
Unlike the other planets in our solar system, Uranus' **axis** points toward the Sun. It is named after the Roman god of the sky.

Earth
The **densest** planet in our solar system, Earth has more water on its surface than land. "Earth" means ground or soil.

How to Draw a
Solar System

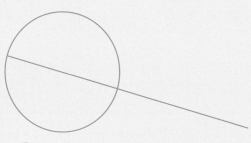

1 Start with a stick figure frame of the solar system. Draw a circle for the Sun, and a line across it.

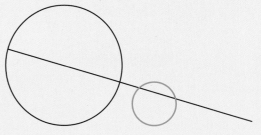

2 Now, draw Jupiter on the line from the previous step.

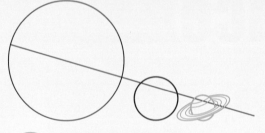

3 Draw Saturn and the ring around it, as shown.

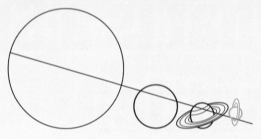

4 Now, using a circle, draw Uranus and the ring around it.

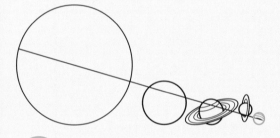

5 In this step, draw Neptune.

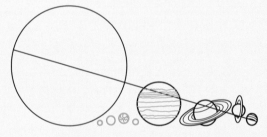

6 Next, add details to Jupiter, and draw Mercury, Venus, Earth and Mars in order from the Sun.

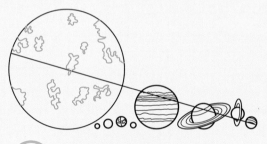

7 Now, draw small curvy figures on the surface of the Sun.

8 Erase the extra lines and the stick figure.

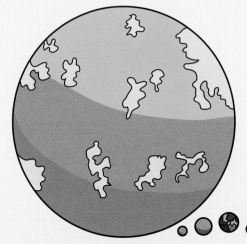

9 Color the picture.

What is a Space Shuttle?

The space shuttle is a type of spaceship built by NASA in the 1980s. It is used to carry people and cargo from the surface of Earth to space. Sometimes, the shuttle links up with the International Space Station. Other times, the shuttle is sent to space to repair a satellite or other spacecraft.

The shuttle is known for its ability to fly into space like a rocket, orbit around Earth like a satellite, and land like an airplane. It can do this because of the way it was built and the parts that make up its construction.

Orbiter
The orbiter is the place where the crew live and work. It has a big bay for carrying cargo into space. The orbiter has three main engines for reaching orbit and wings for returning safely back down through the **atmosphere**.

Payload Doors
The payload doors open to reveal the cargo bay. This is where equipment and machinery, such as satellites, are kept until they are put into space.

External Tank

The external tank carries 528,000 gallons (2.1 million liters) of liquid hydrogen and liquid oxygen as fuel for the engines in the orbiter.

Rocket Booster

The rocket boosters help push the orbiter and the external tank along for the first two minutes of flight. The boosters weigh about 650 tons (590 tonnes).

Main Engines

The shuttle has three main engines that are used once the rocket boosters fall off. They can move the shuttle at speeds of up to 17,000 miles (27,358 kilometers) per hour.

How to Draw a
Space
Shuttle

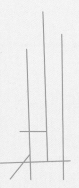

1 Start with a stick figure frame of the space shuttle. Use straight lines to draw the frame.

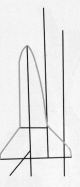

2 Draw the orbiter, as shown.

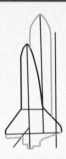

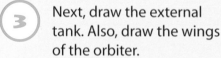

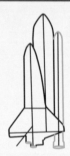

3 Next, draw the external tank. Also, draw the wings of the orbiter.

4 Now, draw one of the rocket boosters, and the thrusters for the orbiter.

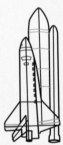

5 In this step, draw the rudder, doors, hatches, and engines of the orbiter.

6 Draw lines on the external tank and wings of the orbiter.

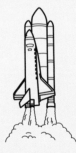

7 Next, draw the other rocket booster, and draw lines on the surface of both the boosters. Also, draw the smoke clouds, as shown.

8 Erase the extra lines and the stick figure.

9 Color the picture.

Test Your Knowledge of Space

1.
The front bubble of an astronaut's helmet is coated in what to filter out the Sun's rays?

Answer: Gold

2.
What are three things a Moon base would need?

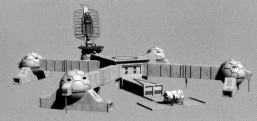

Answer: Housing, laboratories, and lunar vehicles

3.
What was the first rover to land on Mars?

Answer: Sojourner

4.
Name two sources that cause satellites to drift out of place.

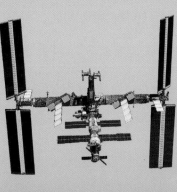

Answer: Solar wind and gravity

5.
How many planets are there in our solar system?

Answer: Eight

6.
How much do a space shuttle's rocket boosters weigh?

Answer: About 650 tons (590 t)

Want to learn more? Log on to av2books.com to access more content.

Draw an Environment

Materials

Large white poster board
Internet connection or library
Pencils and crayons or markers
Glue or tape

Steps

1. Using this book, the internet, and a library, find out what space objects in this book might be found near each other.
2. Go through the book and think of some space objects that fit together. For example, you could have an astronaut working out of a space shuttle or a satellite orbiting a planet.
3. Complete the drawings of the space objects you would like to combine. Cut out the objects.
4. On the large white poster board, draw an environment for your space objects.
5. Place the cutouts in the environment with glue or tape. Color the environment to complete the activity.

Glossary

atmosphere: the layer of gases that surrounds Earth

axis: an imaginary line on which a planet spins

cleats: small spikes that dig into the ground

communication: the sending and receiving of information

densest: packed closely together

gravity: a force that moves things toward the center of a planet

imagination: the ability to form new creative ideas or images

life support: a system that keeps astronauts alive

NASA: National Aeronautics and Space Administration

orbit: to move in a path around a planet or other space object

radio system: a communication system that sends and receives information through electromagnetic waves

space debris: small objects that float in space

terrestrial: from Earth or on Earth

thrusters: a system that creates force to move the shuttle

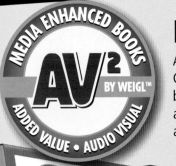

Log on to www.av2books.com

AV² by Weigl brings you media enhanced books that support active learning. Go to www.av2books.com, and enter the special code found on page 2 of this book. You will gain access to enriched and enhanced content that supplements and complements this book. Content includes video, audio, web links, quizzes, a slide show, and activities.

Audio
Listen to sections of the book read aloud.

Video
Watch informative video clips.

Embedded Weblinks
Gain additional information for research.

Try This!
Complete activities and hands-on experiments.

WHAT'S ONLINE?

Try This!	Embedded Weblinks	Video	EXTRA FEATURES
Complete an interactive drawing tutorial for each of the six space objects in the book.	Learn more about each of the six space objects in the book.	Watch a video about space.	**Audio** Listen to sections of the book read aloud. **Key Words** Study vocabulary, and complete a matching word activity. **Slide Show** View images and captions and prepare a presentation **Quizzes** Test your knowledge.

AV² was built to bridge the gap between print and digital. We encourage you to tell us what you like and what you want to see in the future.

Sign up to be an AV² Ambassador at www.av2books.com/ambassador.